ILLEGAL PRAYERS

BOB SORGE

OASIS HOUSE
KANSAS CITY, MO

ILLEGAL PRAYERS

Published by Oasis House
PO Box 522
Grandview, MO 64030-0522
816-767-8880

Editors: Katie Hebbert and Edie Mourey
Cover designer: Joel Sorge
Typesetter: Dale Jimmo

Printed in the United States of America
ISBN: 978-1-937725-33-4
Library of Congress Control Number: 2014951033

For information on all Bob's books, see page 93.

www.oasishouse.com
twitter.com/BOBSORGE
facebook.com/BobSorgeMinistry
Blog: bobsorge.com
To see Bob's films, go to youtube.com, and enter a search for "Bob Sorge Channel"

To Dave & Tracey Sliker, whose friendship has been strengthening and sweet to me, and whose example in pursuing the kingdom of God has inspired thousands. God will surely answer your prayers!

CONTENTS

1. In Pursuit of Answered Prayer 7

2. Painting the Parable's Scenario 19

3 . We Have Laws for This Kind of Behavior 27

4. Disruption 39

5. Relationship Produces Boldness 47

6. Promise Produces Boldness 53

7. Audacity 61

8. Chutzpah! 69

9. A Hearing or a Hanging 83

Ordering Information 93

IN PURSUIT OF ANSWERED PRAYER

God. Answers. Prayer.

From Genesis to Revelation, the Bible is an unbroken series of supernatural interventions. Almost every page in your Bible pulsates with evidence of God's involvement in the affairs of mankind. Clearly, He is eager to be an active participant in our daily lives.

The Bible calls Him, "the God who answers" (1 Kings 18:24). He answers prayer because that's just who He is. He talks. He talks back. He *likes* to talk back. When Paul contrasted the idols of the Gentiles with the Holy Spirit, he described them as "dumb" (1 Cor. 12:1-2)—that is, incapable of talking. Mute. But not our God; when other gods are silent, He hears and responds.

David testified to God's proven record of answering prayer, describing His answers as "benefits."

> Bless the LORD, O my soul, and forget not all His benefits: who forgives all your iniquities, who heals all your diseases, who redeems your life from destruction, who crowns you with lovingkindness and tender mercies, who satisfies your mouth with good things, so that your youth is renewed like the eagle's (Psa. 103:2-5).

This is our God! He saves, heals, delivers, and satisfies. Bless the Lord, O my soul!

When God is quiet, life seems to coast along in its natural order. But when God speaks, stuff happens. Creative forces unleash. Impossibilities materialize. Things buried are suddenly infused with divine life. When God answers prayer, history changes.

When God answers prayer, history changes.

Jesus taught frequently about prayer, and in almost every instance the common thread in His teachings was this: How to receive answers to prayer. Here are just a couple examples.

> So I say to you, ask, and it will be given to you; seek, and you will find; knock, and it will be opened to you. For everyone who asks receives, and he who seeks finds, and to him who knocks it will be opened. If a son asks for bread from any father among you, will he give him a stone? Or if he asks for a fish, will he give him a serpent instead of a fish? Or if he asks for an egg, will he offer him a scorpion? If you then, being evil, know how to give good gifts to your children, how much more will your heavenly Father give the Holy Spirit to those who ask Him! (Luke 11:9-13).

> And whatever you ask in My name, that I will do, that the Father may be glorified in the Son. If you ask anything in My name, I will do it (John 14:13-14).

When you examine Jesus' teachings on prayer, you see how eagerly He labored to show us what it takes to obtain answered prayer.

People of prayer from all centuries have carried Christ's passion for answered prayer. Rees Howells, for example, maintained firmly that the entire meaning and purpose of prayer was to gain the answer.[1] He believed that when God gives a prayer assignment, we must press it all the way through to realization.

Unanswered prayers avail nothing. Effectual prayer is prayer that obtains its object. Over and over, and from many angles, Jesus coached us how to pray our way through to fulfillment.

Why was it so important to Jesus that we touch answered prayer? Let me mention just a few of the many reasons.

1. Answered Prayer Makes the Relationship Real

Jesus wants us to enjoy a relationship with God that is so real, vibrant, and dynamic that it is characterized by answered prayer.

Friendship involves reciprocity. Friendship with God, therefore, is to be a two-way street. There should be give and take—I give to Him, and He gives to me. That's what makes the relationship real.

Unanswered prayers avail nothing.

I will be bold, therefore, and declare that intimacy with God that has no answered prayer is a non-reciprocal relationship. If all my prayer life consists of is telling God how much I love Him, but never receiving back an answer in return, then the relationship is one-sided. And that's not even a real relationship.

You know you're living in intimacy with God when He meets your needs. Let me illustrate what I mean from

1 Norman Grubb, *Rees Howells, Intercessor*; CLC Publications, Fort Washington, PA, 2001, p. 41.

marriage. If my wife were hungry and I gave her affection but no food, I could imagine her questioning the validity of our intimacy. "How can you say our relationship is real when you won't even supply my basic needs?" When intimacy is real, a husband meets his wife's needs for food, clothing, and shelter. Similarly, when our intimacy with God is real, He provides our needs.

James said that faith without works is dead (Jam. 2:26); in a similar sense, intimacy without answered prayer is not true intimacy. We might think it's a living relationship, but it's dead. A living relationship with God must have reciprocity.

My soul longs for the kind of love relationship with my Beloved in which He calls to me, and I answer; then I call to Him, and He answers. *This* is romance!

He calls to me, and I answer; then I call to Him, and He answers.

When God answers your prayer, get ready for your intimacy with Him to go off the charts. As the psalmist said, "I love the LORD, because He has heard my voice and my supplications" (Psa. 116:1). Answers to prayer are like kisses from heaven. They kiss your heart with the assurance of His love. You are struck with how *real* your friendship is.

So let me say it again. Jesus wants us to experience answered prayer as proof that our intimacy with Him is authentic.

2. God is Glorified through Answered Prayer

Another reason Jesus wants us to obtain answered prayers is because they give glory to God. He said so in this passage:

> If you abide in Me, and My words abide in you, you will ask what you desire, and it shall be done for you. By this My Father is glorified (John 15:7-8).

When answered prayer springs from an abiding relationship with Christ, the Father is glorified. Jesus glorified the Father by healing the sick and setting captives free. Similarly, when our connection to Jesus is strong, we will glorify the Father by doing the works He did. Like Master, like disciple. Answered prayer makes you look like Jesus, to the glory of the Father.

Allow the Lord to speak Psalm 50:15 directly to your heart right now. "Call upon Me in the day of trouble; I will deliver you, and you shall glorify Me."

Yes—answered prayer glorifies God.

3. Answered Prayer Stokes Even More Prayer

Another reason Jesus wants us to obtain answered prayer is because it fuels and strengthens our resolve to pray even more. Every answer we receive stokes the furnace of our prayer lives. The psalmist testified to this when he wrote, "Because He has inclined His ear to me, therefore I will call upon Him as long as I live" (Psa. 116:2).

There's a Bible story that beautifully illustrates this idea, and I love the story so much that I must tell it here.

Peter and John were making their way to a prayer meeting in the temple, and on the way they came upon a cripple who was begging for alms. Peter and John didn't have money to give, but they had the power of the Holy Spirit. So they healed the cripple, raised him up, and took him with them to the meeting. He joined them in the temple, "walking, leaping, and praising God" (Acts 3:10).

Some folks, if they had power to raise cripples, would

blow off the prayer meeting. "Why go to a prayer meeting, when we *already* have power to heal the sick?" (As though we pray merely to get power for signs and wonders.) Peter and John weren't going to pray to *get* power to raise cripples; they were going *because* they had power to raise cripples.

Raising the cripple only increased their desire to pray. With the answer to their prayers walking and leaping in their presence, they were eager to join the assembly of believers and revel together in the majesty of Christ. Answered prayer had produced even more prayer.

I consider this a biblically-endorsed way to stoke corporate prayer: When you come across an infirm person, heal them and bring them with you to the prayer meeting. That will put some fresh fire on your worship and intercession!

Here's the point: Answered prayer explosively ignites the flames of prayer. This is why Jesus wants us to obtain answers—He wants us to be empowered and inspired to pray without ceasing.

4. Answered Prayer Invigorates with Boldness

I consider this to be one of the most glorious benefits of answered prayer: It puts boldness in your soul. We see this in Psalm 138:3.

> In the day when I cried out, You answered me, and made me bold with strength in my soul.

In this verse, David described one of the most glorious delights of relationship with God: *same-day answers*. He cried out to God and, before the day was through, God had answered his prayer. Getting an answer so quickly caused David's soul to explode with confidence, making him bold in love and strong in faith.

To every pilgrim reading these words, I want to encourage your prayer journey. *There is a place in God where we experience same-day answers*. Never relax your pilgrimage until you reach that place.

There is a place in God where we experience same-day answers.

Answered prayer is so invigorating (according to Psalm 35:10) that it infuses strength and praise into the very marrow of your bones:

> All my bones shall say, "LORD, who is like You, delivering the poor from him who is too strong for him?"

Jesus delights in the way answered prayer puts boldness and strength in our souls. I will never rest, therefore, until His deliverance causes my entire skeleton to resonate with the cry, "Who is like the Lord?"

UNANSWERED PRAYERS? UNTHINKABLE!

Some world religions have a spiritual culture in which it is considered noble to devote oneself to a lifetime of prayer, even though there is little expectation of ever experiencing an actual answer from heaven. Some of their mystics will spend their entire lives on a mountain or in a temple, devoted to prayer but never hearing back from God.

For us who know the true God and Father of our Lord Jesus Christ, a lifetime of prayer without answers is unthinkable. Intolerable. The essence, meaning, and significance of prayer is *answer*. We devote ourselves to a lifetime of prayer because we know God will answer.

A life of prayer that never receives answers from God is not biblical Christianity. Jesus demonstrated a prayer life in which God always heard and answered (John 11:42). His followers experience the same.

My soul cannot live, therefore, with unanswered prayer. God is too good, and His promises too strong, for me to settle in the bleak badlands of unanswered prayer. Never! It smacks too much of what the prophets of Baal experienced when they called, cried, prophesied, and cut themselves in desperation to get an answer from their god. But the record says, "There was no voice; no one answered, no one paid attention" (1 Kings 18:29). Baal was silent because he could not speak; but should my God also be viewed as mute? Should my God be considered just another Baal who is deaf to prayer? Never! My God and Baal are not peers.

All the religions of the world have one thing in common: unanswered prayer. But us? We serve the one, true, only living God! Answered prayer is one thing that must distinguish our faith from the others. It demonstrates to the world that our gospel is real and true.

My objective in this opening chapter, even before we come to the topic of "Illegal Prayers," is that your soul might ring with the confidence that God answers prayer!

JUST GET IN JESUS' PRESENCE

If you need a prayer answered, all you need to do is get in the immediate presence of Jesus. Because every sick person who came to Him in sincerity, in the Gospel record, received their request. Jesus' earthly ministry demonstrated that if you get in His presence you *will* get your answer. Let me substantiate that with a story from Jesus' life.

News had come to Jesus and the disciples that Lazarus had fallen sick, and Jesus told the disciples that Lazarus was sleeping. The disciples replied, "Surely he'll get better, then." So Jesus told them plainly that Lazarus was dead. And then He uttered these words:

> "And I am glad for your sakes that I was not there, that you may believe" (John 11:15).

Here's what Jesus was implying: "If I had been there when Lazarus had taken sick, they would have asked Me to heal him, and I most certainly would have. But I am glad I was not there because now you will see much more than a healing—you will see a resurrection. And this will bolster your faith."

If Lazarus could have gotten into His presence, he would have been healed. Why? Because Jesus always heals anyone and everyone who comes into His presence and asks for healing.[2]

Get in Jesus' presence and you* will *be healed.

Hear it clearly: Get in Jesus' presence and you *will* be healed. The great challenge, therefore, is to get in His immediate presence. Charles Price wrote of this beautifully when he spoke of meeting the Master in "the garden of answered prayer."[3] He affirmed that there is a

2 The only biblical exception to this was the time when Herod requested a miracle of Jesus (Luke 23:8-9). He brought sick people before Jesus to be healed, but Jesus refused because Herod did it in duplicity, not sincerity. But in every other instance, when people came to Jesus in sincerity, He healed them every time.

3 Charles S. Price, *The Real Faith For Healing*, North Brunswick, NJ: Bridge-Logos Publishers, 1997, p. 4.

place of encounter with Christ where prayers are always answered. This place of encounter is the holy pursuit of the noble soul.

The last chapter of this book will close on this same note. What we seek is an audience with the King. If we can just get into the King's court, we know we will receive the petition we desire of Him. The parable we are about to examine will eventually lead us to the King's court—where He lifts His scepter and receives our request.

Knowing where we will end in this book, let me now explain where we will begin.

LUKE'S TWO PARABLES ON PRAYER

We are about to take an in-depth look at one of Jesus' parables on prayer—the parable in Luke 11:5-8 of the friend who needed three loaves of bread.

Actually, Jesus gave two parables on prayer that are uniquely recorded by Luke. In Luke 11:5-8, He told the parable of the friend who needed bread at midnight. Then, in Luke 18:1-8, He told the parable of the persistent widow who unceasingly cried to her judge for justice from her adversary.

If I were to summarize the message of the parable on the persistent widow, it would be this: How to pray when God is taking a long time to answer. One of the most common questions in our human experience is, "Why does God sometimes take *forever* to answer our prayers?" Jesus' parable in Luke 18 tackles that question head-on. It shows that the delay provides the basis for Him to do much more for us than if He had answered the prayer immediately.

In contrast, I would summarize the message of the

Luke 11 parable in this manner: How to pray when you need an answer *now*.

Both stories look at the diamond of prayer from two vantages that are so different they almost appear paradoxical. Luke 18 prepares us to persevere long-term while the answer is being delayed, while Luke 11 shows us how to receive an immediate answer when a delay simply won't do. To understand the fullness of prayer, we need to see what Jesus was saying in *both* pieces.

The message of the Luke 18 parable has been so significant for me personally that I devoted an entire book to excavating its message—see my book entitled, *Unrelenting Prayer*. And now I devote this present book to the Luke 11 parable. Luke 18 will show you how to posture your heart when God *isn't* answering you right now; Luke 11 will show you how to posture your heart when you *must* have an answer right now.

And yet, even though both parables come at prayer from different angles, the common thread in both is that Jesus is teaching us *how to obtain answers to prayer*.

Do you need an immediate answer from God? Then join me on this quest to meet Christ in the garden of answered prayer. Our guide, from here on, will be the words of Jesus Himself.

PAINTING THE PARABLE'S SCENARIO

Bill's wife, Jen, suddenly came down with cancer. The doctors diagnosed it as an extremely aggressive type of cancer, and Jen was given just weeks to live.

Through previous challenges, Bill had learned how to persevere in faith through a sustained trial. He knew what it was like to be excavated and changed in the refiner's fire, and then to come through, in God's time, to answered prayer. In other words, he was exercised in the kind of faith that waits on God, long-term, until the promise is fulfilled (see Heb. 10:36).

But this was different. This cancer did not provide room for a ten-year journey in God; it was a killer with a very short fuse. They had just weeks. Bill needed to find a different way to pray.

Thankfully, in a parable recorded by Luke, Jesus taught us how to pray in circumstances that necessitate an immediate answer.

"TEACH US TO PRAY"

After Jesus had finished praying in a certain place, His disciples asked Him, "Lord, teach us to pray, as John also taught his disciples" (Luke 11:1). Jesus' prayer life had gripped them with its passion and substance, and they wanted to know how to have the same kind of connection with God.

In response, Jesus gave them the "Our Father" prayer. Then, He immediately launched into a parable. The parable was crafted carefully to illustrate how we should pray. With this parable, Jesus basically said, "I'm glad to answer your question. Let me show you how I pray to the Father."

Some of the implications of this parable are so astonishing they appear almost sacrilegious.

Be warned. Some of the implications of this parable are so astonishing that we might be tempted to consider them almost sacrilegious, except that they came directly from the lips of the Master Himself. So fasten your seatbelt. Jesus is about to teach us how to pray. Here's what He said to His disciples:

> Which of you shall have a friend, and go to him at midnight and say to him, "Friend, lend me three loaves; for a friend of mine has come to me on his journey, and I have nothing to set before him"; and he will answer from within and say, "Do not trouble me; the door is now shut, and my children are with me in bed; I cannot rise and give to you"? I say to you, though he will not rise and give to him because he is his friend, yet because of his persistence he will rise and give him as many as he needs. So I say to you, ask, and it will be given to you; seek, and you will find; knock, and it will be opened to you. For everyone who asks receives, and he who seeks finds, and to him who knocks it will be opened (Luke 11:5-10).

The first thing to observe in Jesus' parable is that its

most prominent word is "friend." It occurs four times. We notice, therefore, that *relationship* is the "root chord" from which all other movements in the parable's symphony spring. You'll miss the melodic nuances of this story unless you see it syncopated throughout with friendship. Two friends are the primary figures, with a third playing a distant role.

Allow me, please, to frame the parable in a contemporary setting. If you'll grant me some literary freedom, here's how the story might look against a modern American backdrop.

Let's say that Jim and Dave are best friends, and they live in Dallas. Furthermore, Jim has another good friend, Chris, who lives in Kansas City. Due to a sudden family situation, Chris needs to make an unexpected trip from Kansas City to Houston. Because of the hurry, everything about his trip is unplanned and somewhat helter-skelter. In the rush, he even forgets his cell phone.

Chris gets away from Kansas City later than he wants, and by the time he nears Dallas, the clock is approaching midnight. He ponders the distance to Houston and groans to himself. He's really tired, and Houston is another four hours away.

Suddenly, he has an inspiration: *Jim! Jim lives in Dallas*. He can stop at Jim's house, get a night's rest, and then head for Houston in the morning. Jumping at the idea, Chris makes his way to Jim's house. By the time he arrives, it's midnight, and the house is black. Everyone is asleep.

Almost apologetically, he knocks on Jim's door and asks if he can spend the night. And the answer, of course, is, "By all means! Come in!"

MIDDLE EASTERN CULTURE

I'm framing the parable in the context of United States geography for the sake of western readers, but in reality the parable was addressed to Jews living in Israel. In the Middle East, if out-of-town company unexpectedly shows up at your doorstep, it goes without saying that you'll lodge them for the night. And the first thing you must do is feed them. Never mind that it's midnight; you don't send your company to bed hungry.

As Jim brings Chris into his small house, everyone wakes up. Jim just goes with the moment and tries to make it appear that he *wants* the family to get up. He tries to make Chris feel totally welcome. "Come on, kids, we have a wonderful surprise. Everybody up, up, up. Come and greet Mr. Chris. He just got here from Kansas City." Jim gathers his wife and kids, seats them at the table with Chris, and gets ready to place some food in front of his friend.

Jim's system is still waking up from a dead sleep. Suddenly, it hits him, "We have no bread!" That evening his family had enjoyed supper with Dave's family at Dave's place, and they didn't bring any leftovers back with them. Everything was left at Dave's house. Jim has no bread in his pantry! *Ugh, what horrible luck! Out of bread—just when company shows up. It's midnight, and the bakery is closed. What am I going to do?*

But then Jim remembers, Dave has bread! After dinner that evening, once the kids had finished playing together and everything had been put away, Jim noticed that Dave had three loaves left over. He watched Dave put them in his pantry. *I'm going to Dave's place,* he thinks to himself, *to get his three loaves of bread for my friend.*

But Jim is too embarrassed to admit to Chris that he

has no food in the house. Chris is already seated at the table with his family, and he'll expect to be fed *something*. So Jim says to Chris and his family, "I've got some food. Hold steady, visit here for a bit, and I'll be right back."

Slipping quickly out the door, Jim runs down the street toward Dave's house. What Jim is about to do—well, let's just say it's not something you do to a neighbor. You do this kind of thing only to a friend. So Jim runs past the homes of several neighbors until he finally gets to his friend's house.

Jim knocks at Dave's door and calls out in a not-so-good whisper, "Dave! Help!"

Dave wakes up to someone knocking on his door. He's disoriented. "Who is it?" he mumbles.

"It's Jim. Dave, I need your help. I need your three loaves of bread."

"What?"

"I said, lend me your three loaves of bread. My buddy Chris just showed up from Kansas City, I wasn't expecting him, and I have no food. Hurry, get out of bed, and get me your three loaves."

"Three loaves? I don't have three loaves."

"Yes, you do. I saw you put them in your pantry after supper. There were leftovers. I saw it. Get up and lend me your three loaves."

By now, Dave is awake and he's starting to think clearly. All he wants is for Jim to go away.

"Shhhh! It's midnight! Are you crazy? Everybody's asleep! Get off my property, go back to bed, and I'll give you the three loaves in the morning."

This is the scenario as Jesus has depicted it, cast in a modern setting. Jim is knocking at Dave's door at midnight, trying to get three loaves of bread so he can feed his buddy Chris who has just shown up from Kansas City.

A LOAN

Before we progress with our story, I want to point to the word "lend" that Jesus used. "Friend, lend me three loaves." In our Dallas setting, Jim asks Dave to "lend" him three loaves.

If Dave agrees to lend him the bread, intrinsic to the loan is the understanding that Jim will now owe him something back. It probably means that Jim's wife will be baking bread first thing in the morning, and then Jim will carry it back to Dave's family.

The idea of "loan" implicitly means that there will be an exchange in the transaction. If Dave gives the loan, Jim will pay something back.

Applied to us, there are times when, in the desperation of our desire to receive an answer from God, we make promissory vows to Him. "God, if You'll just do this one thing for me, then I'll do such-and-such for You." We promise to give Him something back.

He calls to me, and I answer; then I call to Him, and He answers.

This is what Psalm 65:1 is pointing to: "Praise is awaiting You, O God, in Zion; and to You the vow shall be performed." David was saying, "You know the vow I've made to You; when You answer me, I will give back to You the thing I have vowed and I will praise You for Your goodness."

There are some situations in which, after you receive

what you desire from God, you will carry a sense of indebtedness to Him. He has done such wonderful things for you that now you will do whatever is necessary to return the debt of love you owe.

That's the significance I see in the word "lend." When He answers our prayer, we'll owe Him. Now let's move forward with the scene.

WE HAVE LAWS FOR THIS KIND OF BEHAVIOR

Look more closely at verse 5 of Luke 11.

> Which of you shall have a friend, and go to him at midnight and say to him, "Friend, lend me three loaves."

Our parable is in black and white until you see two words that turn it into technicolor. The first kaleidoscopic word is *midnight*. To grasp the story, you've got to see the entire proceedings shaking down at *midnight*. Everything in the vignette is unplanned, inconvenient, and ill-timed for everybody.

When Jim first shows up at Dave's door, knocks, and asks for bread, he's not doing anything wrong. It's permissible to knock on someone's door. Once. But when Dave says, "It's midnight. Shut up, get off my property and go back to bed," and Jim continues to knock and call out, we have laws for this kind of behavior. We call it trespassing. Harassment. Disturbing the peace. Once Dave says, "Get off my property," and Jim continues to stand at midnight and call for assistance, he is now breaking the law.

I am not stretching the parable to suggest Jim is breaking the law. If you don't think this is illegal behavior, then go ahead and give it a shot. Go down the road, knock at somebody's door at midnight, refuse to get off their property, and see what happens. You may find yourself in handcuffs.

Jesus could have put the parable at another time of day, such as high noon, but by placing it at midnight He subtly designed an illegal setting. When you see that Jesus positioned Jim to be breaking the law, you realize He was actually advocating *illegal prayers*.

Jesus was actually advocating illegal prayers.

Jim is now violating city ordinances. In a very real sense, he is serving his friend Dave an ultimatum. "I'm not going anywhere, so you have a choice. Call the cops, or give me your three loaves."

But Jim is thinking to himself, *I don't think you're going to call the cops. Our friendship is too strong. Our families are too close. We've known each other for too many years. Before you call the cops, I think you're going to drag your carcass out of bed, go to your pantry, and get your three loaves.*

Jim is now putting pressure on the relationship. He's about to discover if their friendship can sustain this kind of strain or if it will break. Jim is wondering, *Are you just a fairweather friend? Are you my friend only when things are great, or are you also my friend when things are hard?*

By straining the relationship, Jim is drawing on his relational equity with Dave. He's about to find out whether he's accrued enough collateral in their relational bank to cash in on it in a time of need.

Illegal prayers leverage relational equity.

Relational equity is earned through time spent together and favors done for each other. Jim has undoubtedly done many little favors for Dave over the years, and now he has the boldness to expect a favor in return. In terms of our relationship with Christ, this reminds me of 1 Timothy 3:13, "For those who have served well as deacons obtain for themselves a good standing and great boldness in the faith which is in Christ Jesus." When we are faithful in our service for Christ, we gain the boldness to pray audacious prayers in our time of need.

Jim felt secure enough in his friendship with Dave to demand assistance in a way that actually broke the law. In a similar sense, if you're going to pray illegal prayers, you better have a friendship with God. Don't wait for a crisis to hit before you start investing in your relationship with God. Build relational equity with God *now*, so that when the crisis hits you have a friendship to fall back on.

Illegal prayers leverage relational equity.

Just because you're bold in the presence of God does not mean you're a spoiled brat with a spirit of entitlement; it means you're someone who has confidence in your beloved Friend.

Confidence will say to God, "If You say no, I'm not leaving. If You say later, I'm not leaving. The only way I'll quiet down is if You give me Your three loaves."

Illegal prayers are rooted in the relational confidence of knowing your God and, even better, being known by Him. You can have enough confidence in your friendship to believe that ever before He gets angry and swats you into outer space, He's going to give you the healing bread He has in His heavenly pantry.

The title of this book—Illegal Prayers—wasn't chosen because I thought it was a clever title. I chose it because of what's going on in the parable. Jim is praying illegal prayers at Dave's door. But Jesus' parable is not the only instance of illegal prayers in the Bible. There are a few others.

HANNAH

Hannah could not have children, and it vexed her soul greatly. Consumed with longing to have a child, she went into the house of the Lord and began to pour out her heart in prayer. Finally, in the anguish and desperation of her soul, she said, "O LORD of hosts, if You will indeed look on the affliction of Your maidservant and remember me, and not forget Your maidservant, but will give Your maidservant a male child, then I will give him to the LORD all the days of his life" (1 Sam. 1:11).

She was so desperate for a son that she said, "If You give me a son, I'll give Him back to You." And as the story turned out, she gave birth to a son whom she turned over to Eli, the priest. Thus, her son Samuel was raised in the house of the Lord by Eli.

Was Hannah's prayer legal? Is it permissible to abandon your child like that? How about "abandonment" laws? True, she gave him to the care of another; but Eli wasn't that great of a caretaker. He had a poor record with his own sons, so what made him fit to be a father to Samuel?

At the least, the story is unconventional. And yet, God used Hannah's barrenness—and the desperate cry her barrenness generated—to answer her prayer and give her a son. The cry of a desperate mother enabled

God to procure, in Samuel, the prophet He needed to transition the nation of Israel from the era of the judges to the era of the kings.

DANIEL

In the days when Babylon was the ruling world empire, Babylon invaded Israel and took Daniel, along with many other Jews, back to Babylon. Because of his wisdom, Daniel was promoted to a place of political prominence in the kingdom. Later, when Babylon was conquered by Persia, Daniel continued to serve in a place of eminence in the empire. He had so much favor with the king that the princes of Persia grew envious.

The princes conspired a way to get rid of Daniel. Under false pretenses, they convinced the king to enact a decree that no one be allowed to pray to any god but the king for thirty days (see Daniel 6). If someone prayed to another, they were to be thrown into the lion's den.

As soon as Daniel learned that this legislation had been signed into law by the king, he went to his home, opened his window toward Jerusalem, and prayed to his God. He would allow nothing to stop his practice of praying three times a day to the God of Israel. If he could no longer pray legal prayers, then he would pray illegal prayers.

If he could no longer pray legal prayers, then Daniel would pray illegal prayers.

And his illegal prayers got him into serious trouble. He was arrested and thrown into the lion's den. But God stood by His man, sent His angel, and shut the mouths of the lions. What started as illegal prayers ended in a mighty deliverance.

ISAIAH

In the book of Isaiah, God invited us to pray in a manner that strikes the reader as illegal or, at the very least, irreverent.

> Thus says the LORD, the Holy One of Israel, and his Maker: "Ask Me of things to come concerning My sons; and concerning the work of My hands, you command Me" (Isa. 45:11).

Some translations have reworded the verse to make it more palatable, but our translation here is altogether accurate. God is actually inviting His servants to *command* Him to do what they want.

Commanding God? Isn't that presumptuous and arrogant?

Commanding God? Telling God what to do? Isn't that presumptuous, arrogant, and disrespectful of His sovereignty? Isn't that kind of praying illegal?

THE OVERCROWDED HOUSE

Here's another story that somehow seems to be suspiciously unlawful:

> And again He entered Capernaum after some days, and it was heard that He was in the house. Immediately many gathered together, so that there was no longer room to receive them, not even near the door. And He preached the word to them. Then they came to Him, bringing a paralytic who was carried by four men. And when they could not come near Him because of the crowd, they

> uncovered the roof where He was. So when they had broken through, they let down the bed on which the paralytic was lying. When Jesus saw their faith, He said to the paralytic, "Son, your sins are forgiven you." And some of the scribes were sitting there and reasoning in their hearts, "Why does this Man speak blasphemies like this? Who can forgive sins but God alone?" But immediately, when Jesus perceived in His spirit that they reasoned thus within themselves, He said to them, "Why do you reason about these things in your hearts? Which is easier, to say to the paralytic, 'Your sins are forgiven you,' or to say, 'Arise, take up your bed and walk'? But that you may know that the Son of Man has power on earth to forgive sins"—He said to the paralytic, "I say to you, arise, take up your bed, and go to your house." Immediately he arose, took up the bed, and went out in the presence of them all, so that all were amazed and glorified God, saying, "We never saw anything like this!" (Mark 2:1-12).

We know that Jesus broke many rules of His day. He ate with unwashed hands; He allowed His disciples to pick and eat grain on the Sabbath; He told a cripple to carry his bed on the Sabbath, etc. But in this story, He broke one of *my* rules! I have a rule that says you must repent before you can be forgiven. But here, Jesus forgives a man who didn't even repent of his sins. Can you do that? Is that legal?

Furthermore, the four men who brought him to Jesus broke the law. Folks, you can't just take apart somebody's roof, even if your motives are noble. Call it breaking and entering. Call it vandalism. Whatever you want to call it, it's illegal.

But Jesus called it faith. And healed the man.

WOMAN WITH A HEMORRHAGE

Here's still another biblical instance where laws were broken. There was a woman in Israel who had a problem in her reproductive organs that precipitated ongoing blood loss. None of the physicians she consulted could staunch the flow of blood; instead, her condition grew worse.

One day she heard that Jesus of Nazareth would be passing through town. *Jesus! The Son of God! The Healer! It's now or never.* Faith filled her heart. *If I could just touch the hem of His garment, I know that would be enough. I know I would be healed of this infirmity.*

But there was a problem. The law of Moses commanded that anyone with this kind of bodily discharge live sequestered and isolated from the community (Num. 5:2). Such a person was ceremonially "unclean," meaning they were prohibited from coming into the temple to worship while thus defiled. Furthermore, Moses' law explained that, if a person who was unclean because of a hemorrhage touched someone else, the other person would be defiled by that touch and rendered ceremonially unclean as well—that is, unable to worship in the temple until ceremonially cleansed (Lev. 15:19). God considered it unjust for an unclean person to defile others through physical contact, even though their personal problem was unfortunate. So He passed a law stipulating that an unclean person must be quarantined from others until cured.

The law, therefore, prohibited this woman from mixing in public places. And yet, Jesus was thronged by multitudes. How could she possibly touch the hem of His garment when He was surrounded by such masses? Furthermore, everyone in town knew she lived in seclusion because of uncleanness. If they saw her in the crowd, they would thrust her out immediately. What could she possibly do to get within touching distance of Jesus?

She grabbed a shawl, draped it across her shoulders, and pulled it down over her head. Then bending low so that her face was not visible to anyone, she began to shove her way through the crowd.

As she pushed through the legs of the crowd, she might have whispered, "Excuse me," under her breath. Each person she wiggled past and brushed against was defiled by her physical contact. "Excuse me, sorry about that." She wasn't meaning to defile others; she simply had no other option. "Pardon me, sorry about that." But she continued to push and shove her way to Jesus.

By the time she got to Jesus, she had broken the law some 235 times (or however many people she had touched on her way to Jesus). That's why, when Jesus called out, "Who touched My clothes?" she trembled in fear and tried to hide. She didn't want to be exposed as having violated Moses' law countless times in order to receive her healing.

What kind of faith is so bold that it is willing to defile even the Son of God Himself in order to get an answer?

When she could hide no longer, she fell before Jesus and told Him everything. How did Jesus respond to her illegal quest? He said to her, "Daughter, your faith has made you well. Go in peace, and be healed of your affliction" (Mark 5:34).

What kind of faith is so bold that it is willing to defile even the Son of God Himself in order to get an answer?

This woman knew that to touch His garment, she would have to push past a crowd of opinions. So will you. There are all kinds of rational voices that will try to talk you out of pushing through to Jesus' hem.

"You deserve hell, so just be thankful for what you've got."

"He's already done so much for you, if He never does another thing for you, it's more than enough."

"You just need to focus on giving glory to God, whether by life or by death."

"This is not about you."

I agree with all of you. You have great theology. But get out of my way. I've got to touch Jesus!

JESUS ADVOCATES ILLEGAL PRAYERS

These examples of illegal prayers in the Bible serve to substantiate the scenario Jesus painted in Luke 11 with our fictitious characters, Jim and Dave. By having Jim on Dave's doorstep at midnight and refusing to remove himself—which is against the law—Jesus was advocating illegal prayers. Jesus was intimating, "You have a relationship with God. Go for broke. Break the law. Forget the rules. Push the envelope. Violate protocol. Brook no denial. Demand attention."

Go for broke.

Jesus' message here is quite startling. "You're a beloved friend—a child of God. So ditch propriety. Go for the jugular. Call the question. Press the point. Strain the relationship. Despise political correctness. Contravene convention. Test the limits. Cross the line. Throw caution to the wind. Pray illegal prayers."

When you go to offering such bold prayers, you might want to keep your voice down—because if someone overhears your prayer, he might step aside, fearing a lightning strike. "You're not supposed to talk to God like that!"

But that eavesdropper is not the one with whom you have this friendship, and he's not the one to whom you're praying. So just move yourself out of his earshot, and talk to your Friend.

DISRUPTION

We're going to push deeper into our parable now, so please allow me to quote it again.

> Which of you shall have a friend, and go to him at midnight and say to him, "Friend, lend me three loaves; for a friend of mine has come to me on his journey, and I have nothing to set before him"; and he will answer from within and say, "Do not trouble me; the door is now shut, and my children are with me in bed; I cannot rise and give to you"? (Luke 11:5-7).

Dave says, "My children are with me in bed," and here's why. In Jesus' day, houses were small and typically had just one bedroom. Everyone in the house slept in the same room. If one person got up, chances are that others would be roused. Dave doesn't want to awaken his children.

Everything in the house is black because of the hour. He could bump into a couple of the kids by accident while crawling over them. Or, he could make noise in the pantry while searching and fumbling around for the loaves. Plus, there's the sound of the door opening and closing. Chances are likely that if he gets up to get bread for Jim, the kids will awaken.

The big issue for Dave, therefore, is disruption. If his

kids wake up, that will disturb everything.

We all know that when your children are asleep, they're angels. And if you awaken them in the middle of the night, they're demons.

"Don't wake up my kids!" Dave huffs in Jim's direction. "Your timing is horrible. I'd like to help, but my kids are with me in bed, and if they wake up everything will be disrupted. So get off my property, go back to bed, and come back in the morning."

Answered prayers are disruptive.

In the parable, Jim calls Dave his buddy, but Dave doesn't echo the same warmth. Right now, Dave is too frustrated to call Jim his friend. He just wants Jim to go away because of the disruption factor.

The fact is, answered prayers are disruptive. They disrupt the normal course of life and accelerate kingdom activity in the earth. Dave represents God in the parable, and Dave's disruption points to how God is disrupted by answered prayer. And in some respects, so are we. If you think that everything associated with answered prayer is pleasant and jolly, think again. Answered prayer sometimes opens the door to difficulty.

This is why Jesus, when He healed and delivered people, would often plead, "Don't tell anybody about this!" The more attention His supernatural ministry received, the sooner He'd be crucified. Every miracle escalated the domino effect toward Calvary. For Jesus, miracles meant trouble.

For example, consider the raising of Lazarus from the dead. If I were Jesus, I probably would have been thinking something like, *Guys, this is going to be a good one. This one is going to* really *wow you*. I would have had adrenalin pumping through my veins in anticipation. But it wasn't like that for Jesus. He was probably thinking, "This one is going to be *really* troublesome for Me. This one is going to get Me crucified." It was the raising of Lazarus that caused Jesus' enemies to ramp up their conspiracy efforts.

Answered prayers are disruptive and troublesome. They accelerate world history. Current political upheavals illustrate this principle. At the time of this writing, there is political disruption in Ukraine, Iraq, Syria, Gaza, and Libya (to name just a few nations). Those seedbeds of turmoil actually accelerate change in the nations. As we watch the news, we feel like we're watching human history hasten toward the culmination of all things.

Disruption accelerates. This is why answered prayers are so disruptive to God—they accelerate the chain of end-time events that catapult us toward the return of Christ.

Answered prayers accelerate world history.

I can suppose God thinking, *I'm not ready to answer your prayer right now. Don't get Me wrong, I* will *answer your prayer; but not just yet. If I deliver you right now, it would disrupt too many things. I've got a timetable for this planet. Everything is intentional and deliberate. I'm planning for world history to culminate in a way that follows a purposeful, clear blueprint. So keep praying, keep calling on Me, keep pressing into the kingdom; but give Me some time, I'm not ready yet to tip the domino by answering your prayer.*

When God is saying, "Too disruptive," Jesus' counsel to us in the parable is quite stunning. He is basically saying, "Challenge God's sovereignty." When God says, "Not now," Jesus advises us to push back. "God, I know You have a cosmic plan. I know that You have an entire world to manage, and answering me right now might disrupt Your global timelines. But I don't care. You've got what I need, and I won't back down."

It's in this spirit that I can hear Jim saying to Dave, "I'm sorry, Buddy, that this is disruptive to you. I realize this will awaken your entire family. I feel badly about that. But hey—I'm disrupted too! My wife and kids are all awake, seated around my kitchen table with my guest, and waiting for me to bring some food. You don't want to be disrupted? Well, I'm *already* disrupted. So pull yourself over to your pantry and lend me your three loaves!"

Can we really challenge God's sovereignty? Let me explain. Jesus is not suggesting we should challenge God's sovereign wisdom or sovereign purposes. But He is coaching us to challenge God's sovereign *timing*. When we know what God intends to do, we can push back on His sovereignty and call for *a sooner fulfillment* of His sovereign plans.

There is a kind of praying that receives today what God was intending to do tomorrow.

There is a kind of praying that receives today what God was intending to do tomorrow. And here's the stunning part: It's God Himself who is coaching us to pray this way.

Somebody needs to say to God, "I realize that, when

You perform this miracle, it will trigger things in the Spirit realm that will disrupt and accelerate Your plans for this region. But I don't care. We're *already* disrupted down here. So answer our prayer *now*. Feed us from the bread in Your heavenly pantry!"

KINGDOM VIOLENCE

There's an element of violence in this kind of praying—the kind of violence that Jesus espoused in Matthew 11:12—"And from the days of John the Baptist until now the kingdom of heaven suffers violence, and the violent take it by force." One of the implications of this statement seems to be that something changed with the ministry of John the Baptist.

Prior to John, there was a kind of spiritual violence that was not practiced or at least not recognized. It doesn't seem that the Old Covenant endorsed the challenging of God's sovereignty. But something changed with the advent of the gospel. Jesus announced that the kingdom of God now permitted and even invited a kind of spiritual violence that was formerly not allowed.

In the kingdom, we are invited to a kind of spiritual violence that actually refuses to settle for providential timing, and lays claim to kingdom provisions *now*.

My friend, Bill Farina, told me that he sees a progression of intensity in prayer in Jesus' words in Luke 11:9-10, "Ask...seek...knock." He put it this way: Suppose you lose your keys. At first, you *ask* everyone around you if they've seen them. Then you start to *seek* in corners and crevices and under cushions. As the search grows in desperation, you begin to *knock* things over. In other words, there's aggression in the kind of prayer that Jesus counsels.

As Joseph Garlington has said, "You've got to go to the mat with God."

IN THE PRESENCE OF THE FAMILY

In the parable, Jim seems intent upon appealing to Dave in the presence of his family. It wouldn't be long before Dave's family would begin to stir due to the commotion. The kids are going to hear Jim outside, pleading with their father, "Give me your three loaves!"

But Dave is grumpy. He doesn't want to get out of bed. And he doesn't want his kids to wake up.

At some point, Dave's wife and kids are going to start waking up and tuning into what's happening. "Dad's friend is at the door, pleading for bread, and Dad is being real grumpy and abrupt with him."

It's not long before the kids view their Dad as the bad guy in the situation.

"Dad! Why are you acting this way? Why are you snubbing your friend? All he's asking for is three little loaves. My goodness, Dad, he's your *friend*. And you have the bread. Give it to him!"

By saying to their dad, "I can't believe you're acting this way," the kids are adding to the pressure Dave feels to get out of bed.

And for his part, Jim is quite happy for the kids to put some pressure on their dad. "Let the family put the screws on you, that's fine with me. I just need your bread."

Here's the point. If you need something from God, lift your voice in the presence of His kids.

CLICHÉS

When we consider the bold manner in which Jesus is teaching us to pray in this parable, it causes us to question some of the pious clichés that we sometimes use in our prayers to God.

"If it be Thy will."[1]

Dave's answer to Jim is, "I'll tell you my will. Shut up, get off my property, and go back to bed."

"In Your perfect time and in Your perfect way."

"I'll tell you my perfect time," Dave retorts. "8:00 a.m.! Come back at 8:00 a.m. and I'll gladly give you my bread in the morning."

But Jim is going to push back. "I don't need your bread at 8:00 a.m. The *bakery* is open at 8:00 a.m. Man, *my wife* can bake fresh bread at 8:00 a.m. But that doesn't help me now. Chris is seated at my table with my family, waiting for bread. No, I need bread *now*!"

Yes, God is sovereign. We must never lose our honor and respect for the wisdom of His sovereign plans in the earth. But if your relationship with Him is real, and you need an answer *now*, then press Him!

That said, let me acknowledge the balancing truth of Luke 18:1-8. In the matching parable of Luke 18, Jesus teaches us to wait on God in prayer until He answers. I believe in waiting on God. I have written ~~entire books~~ on the subject. But waiting on God is not sitting by the pool, sipping on lemonade, and hanging out until God gets around to doing something. Waiting on God is anything but laid-back and passive. Waiting on God is possibly one of the most violent things you'll ever do. Here's

1 To clarify my meaning, I do believe there are unique times when it's fitting to pray, "If it be Thy will." In Gethsemane, Jesus said to His Father, "Nevertheless, not what I will, but what You will" (Mk. 14:36). We also have Gethsemane moments—times when we likewise surrender ourselves to God's will. Not every situation in life, however, corresponds to Christ's altar of surrender in Gethsemane. In some situations, "If it be Thy will" is simply an empty cliché that reflects our timidity and unbelief.

how I define waiting on God: Putting pressure on the kingdom of God.

Press! Push back! Challenge God's sovereign timing! These are the astounding implications of Jesus' teaching here. Dispense with polite courtesies, and let your requests be made known to God.

Press! Push back! Challenge God's sovereign timing!

Here's a cliché I hear quite often from other people, when they comment about the healing that I myself need. They sometimes say to me, "Well, Bob, you're going to be healed—if not on this side of the veil, then on the other side."

But I don't need healing on the other side of the veil. I need healing *now*!

RELATIONSHIP PRODUCES BOLDNESS

In our parable, Jim is exercising uncommon boldness with Dave because of their relationship. In this chapter, I want to illustrate even further how relationship produces boldness in prayer. To demonstrate that principle, let's turn aside from our parable and look at the example of Mary, the mother of Jesus.

There's a story in Mary's life that displays the boldness she had in her relationship with Jesus. The incident I have in mind is when Jesus turned water into wine. At the time of this wedding, it's clear that Jesus had already started his teaching ministry. But He had not yet launched His miraculous ministry. The story upon which we now draw tells how His miraculous ministry was triggered:

> On the third day there was a wedding in Cana of Galilee, and the mother of Jesus was there. Now both Jesus and His disciples were invited to the wedding. And when they ran out of wine, the mother of Jesus said to Him, "They have no wine." Jesus said to her, "Woman, what does your concern have to do with Me? My hour has not yet come." His mother said to the servants, "Whatever He says to you, do it." Now there were set there six waterpots of stone, according to the manner of purification of the Jews, containing twenty or thirty gallons

> apiece. Jesus said to them, "Fill the waterpots with water." And they filled them up to the brim. And He said to them, "Draw some out now, and take it to the master of the feast." And they took it. When the master of the feast had tasted the water that was made wine, and did not know where it came from (but the servants who had drawn the water knew), the master of the feast called the bridegroom. And he said to him, "Every man at the beginning sets out the good wine, and when the guests have well drunk, then the inferior. You have kept the good wine until now!" This beginning of signs Jesus did in Cana of Galilee, and manifested His glory; and His disciples believed in Him (John 2:1-11).

When Mary said to Jesus, "They have no wine," Jesus did what He always did. He checked in with His Father. "Abba? How about it? Want Me to do something here?"

The Father's response must have been something like, "Not now. Too disruptive. Once You perform that first sign, there will be no going back. The domino will be tipped, and the miracles will increasingly cascade and tumble, hastening Your course toward Calvary. I'm just not ready for all of that to start yet. It's premature. Let's hold off for now."

Can you really be at a standoff with Almighty God and get what you want?

So Jesus turned to His mother and said, "My hour has not yet come." What He meant was, "The hour for my supernatural ministry is not here yet. It's just not the right time for that."

But Mary wasn't about to accept no for an answer. She decided to push back. "We don't need wine tomorrow," I can suppose her saying to Jesus. "The wedding's not tomorrow, it's today. We need wine *now*." So she immediately said to the servants, "Whatever He says to you, do it."

When I look at what Mary did here, it seems illegal to me. She was basically at loggerheads with Abba Father. The Father was saying, "Not now," and Mary was saying, "Now." Can you really be at a standoff with Almighty God and get what you want?

Mary decided to exercise her maternal authority. "You know that Scripture says children are to honor their father *aaaaand* their mother!"

Relationship made her bold.

Mary decided to leverage her relationship with Jesus. I can imagine her wondering, "How much emotional capital do I have with You, anyways? I conceived You, carried You, pushed You into the world, nursed You, changed You, fed You, clothed You, protected You, trained You, and raised You. You Yourself know that our relationship is special. We've shared a strong history together. Now that I need something from You, can I draw on our relational equity?"

Relationship made her bold.

Jesus' mother and Father were at odds on the matter, and Jesus was caught in the middle. He looked over at His mother; then He looked up at His Father; then back to His mother; then back again to His Father. "What am I supposed to do? Abba, look at her. She's using the mother card."

It's as though Abba shrugged and said, "Yeah, I know. What can You do?"

And Mary got her wine.

But she did more than just get an abundance of wine. She actually activated the advent of Christ's supernatural ministry. What's really stunning is that she triggered it *before its time*. It was certainly due to come, but not just yet—until Mary got into the mix, that is. She participated in what Peter later called, "hastening the coming of the day of God" (2 Pet. 3:12). What Mary did was epochal. She initiated, through her audacity, a new era in God's calendar.

And all because she needed wine *now*.

I can suppose God saying over some parts of the earth today, "I'm definitely going to send revival to your land. You've been praying and crying out to Me, and I'm going to do it. But not just yet. I'm lining things up. I've got things happening in China, in Australia, in Europe, in Brazil—I've got a whole globe to consider and manage. So keep praying, but bear up just a little bit longer, I'm not ready to tip the domino just yet. It would be too disruptive right now."

There's a generation that will push back and say, "We can't live with that. We need the wine of revival *now*."

ACCELERATING THE TIMING

The timing of God's interventions in the earth is one of the most cloudy, opaque dynamics of the kingdom for us to see and know. It's just downright difficult to discern God's timing on things. It's much easier to see the "what" than the "when." Peter pointed to this when he said the prophets of old peered with all their strength to see, not only *what* God was planning to do, but *when* it would happen (see 1 Pet. 1:11). We face the same struggle. There are some things we know God is going to do;

we just can't perceive when He intends to do them.

You might know what God is going to do, but until you know the timing of it, the thing remains locked up and hidden to you.

The saints have always wrestled with God's timing on things. Bible writers often asked questions like, "When? How long?" Many times they cried out, "Do not delay!" For example, when John saw the fifth seal being opened, he heard the martyrs under the altar in heaven crying aloud to God, "How long, O Lord, holy and true, until You judge and avenge our blood on those who dwell on the earth?" (Rev. 6:10). They were not crying out for God to avenge their blood—they knew He was going to. What they didn't know was the timing. By crying, "How long?" they were pushing and contending for an acceleration of that which was most certainly to come.

Mary's example reveals that we have divine permission to challenge God's sovereign timing.

It's this same kind of pressing and contending that Mary embodied. She was resolved to push on the timing of Jesus' miraculous ministry, and she received a miracle before Jesus' time for miracles had come. Her example demonstrates that there is a way in the kingdom to accelerate the timing of what God intends to do in the earth.

If you're looking at something that God has no intention of doing, then you can't accelerate it through your boldness. Your audacity can't procure something that is against God's will. But if it's within His will, and you know it's just a matter of time before He does it, then Mary's example tells us we can put pressure on God's timetable.

I find this principle stunning. Mary's example reveals that we have divine permission to challenge God's sovereign timing.

Do you hold a promise from God? Is there something that you know He plans to do, but you just don't know His holy timing? You have permission from heaven to strive with God for a sooner fulfillment. Lean on that promise, plead that promise, and push in the Spirit for an early release.

If you, like Mary, have an invested relationship with Jesus, you just might get your wine before it's time.

PROMISE PRODUCES BOLDNESS

The previous chapter showed how we have divine permission, when holding a promise from God, to contend with God for an early fulfillment. In this chapter, I want to expand even further on the manner in which promise makes us bold. Chase a trail with me for this chapter, please, and then we will return to our Luke 11 parable.

One of the most valuable things you can have in this life is a promise from God. God's promises are "exceedingly great and precious" (2 Pet. 1:4) because they are guarantees that, before our story is finished, God is going to visit us with His power and fulfill the promise. The promise is so laden with power that it will carry us until the day of breakthrough.

When God has not yet answered, we get discouraged all too easily with the delay. What we sometimes fail to fully appreciate is the amazing treasure we actually have in our possession—a promise from God.

The first thing I want to say to you if you have a promise from God is this: Do everything in your power to keep your fingers wrapped around that promise! It's just too precious to lose.

When holding to promise for a long time, we're often

tempted to lose heart and relinquish our hope. The reason it's so imperative to hold to hope is this: Jettisoned promises can be lost forever. Not every promise is unconditional. Some must be carried tenaciously if they are to be fulfilled. We see this truth in these verses:

> Do not become sluggish, but imitate those who through faith and patience inherit the promises (Heb. 6:12).
>
> And let us not grow weary while doing good, for in due season we shall reap if we do not lose heart (Gal. 6:9).
>
> Therefore do not cast away your confidence, which has great reward. For you have need of endurance, so that after you have done the will of God, you may receive the promise (Heb. 10:35-36).

Holding onto promise can be likened, in a figurative sense, to the way a wide receiver cradles a football. After he catches the ball, he pulls it close to his body, sets his eyes on the goal line and resolves within himself, *No matter what happens during this run, I must not let go this ball!* In the same way, we must resolve intently to hold fast our confidence.

My soul refuses to live in the badlands of abandoned promises.

I can hardly imagine anything more tragic than to receive a promise from God but then fumble it because it wasn't fulfilled in my timing. To once have a promise, but now be without it, is like subsisting in a wasteland of heartsick hopelessness.

My soul refuses to live in the badlands of abandoned promises. I am resolved to do whatever I must to keep His promise close to my heart. Fasting, prayer, and word immersion are gifts from God to empower us to maintain our grip on His promise.

When you have a promise firmly in your possession, an uncommon boldness and confidence overtakes your soul. The unfulfilled promise means that it must be fulfilled in your lifetime (because God's word does not return to Him void, Isaiah 55:11). That confidence infuses your soul with boldness concerning the present. Present circumstances cannot annul your promise.

Let me illustrate how promise produces boldness with some biblical examples.

ABRAHAM

Abraham was promised by God that he would become a great nation (Gen. 12:2), which meant that he would have at least one son. But at the time, he had no children because his wife, Sarah, was barren. If Abraham was to become a great nation, God would have to perform a miracle in their childless marriage. God's promise meant, by implication, that God was going to give them a miracle baby.

A few years later, while Sarah still had no son, Abraham's nephew, Lot, was taken captive by invaders. A federation of foreign armies had taken Lot and his entire city captive (Gen. 14:14). In response, Abraham mobilized all the manpower he could muster—318 men. In contrast to the forces in the foreign alliance, Abraham's militia was quickly thrown together. The odds were stacked miserably against him and his tiny band of warriors. But he had an unfulfilled promise from God, and that promise had placed a boldness in his soul. That boldness enabled him to step forward audaciously and engage the enemy.

Guess who won? The man who carried a promise. I mean, think about it. How could a legion of foreign armies kill a man who possessed an unfulfilled promise? Not possible.

How could a legion of foreign armies kill a man who possessed an unfulfilled promise?

CALEB

When the nation of Israel came from Egypt to the border of Canaan, Moses sent twelve men into Canaan to spy out the land and bring back a report. Ten of them brought back an evil report, saying that the land could not be conquered. Only Caleb and Joshua asserted with confidence that God would enable them to take the land.

In response to Caleb's faith, God promised that he would possess Mount Hebron (Josh. 14:12-14), which was the area of Canaan that Caleb had personally scouted (Josh. 14:9). As it turned out, he had to hold this promise for forty-five years before it would be fulfilled.

It was the promise of Hebron that empowered Caleb to endure forty years of trekking through the wilderness. What's more, that promise also preserved his body so that at age eighty-five he had the strength and energy of a forty-year-old (Josh. 14:11). God preserved his strength so he could take and inhabit the promise given him forty-five years earlier.

Let me ask you a question. How could a flea-infested, scorpion-enhanced, viper-ridden, dust-filled, sunbaked desert take out a man who had an unfulfilled promise? Not possible.

DAVID

When Samuel found David and anointed him with oil, he told him that God had anointed him to be king over the nation of Israel (1 Sam. 16:13). That promise put brash boldness into David's spirit, so much so that he went up against Goliath, a seasoned champion of the Philistine army (1 Sam. 17:48).

In the natural, everything was stacked against David. Goliath was older, taller, stronger, more trained, and much more battle experienced. All David had was a promise and a sling.

And he bested the giant. Promise had spurred him to take on an audacious duel with preposterous odds because he knew the promise must be fulfilled.

Let me ask you a question. How could a Spirit-led man of faith who carries a powerful promise be taken out prematurely by an uncircumcised Philistine? Not possible.

JEHOSHAPHAT

While Jehoshaphat was king of Judah, a coalition of armies came from the direction of Syria to conquer Judah and Jerusalem. In response, Jehoshaphat called a national fast, gathered the people to Jerusalem, and urged them to seek the Lord's favor and help.

When the people had congregated, Jehoshaphat led in prayer. He reminded God of His promises to the nation. "We have no power against this great multitude that is coming against us," he said to the Lord, "Nor do we know what to do, but our eyes are upon You" (2 Chron. 20:12).

After Jehoshaphat had humbled himself and called on the Lord, the Spirit of God fell on Jahaziel, one of the

Levites in the assembly, and he began to prophesy: "The battle is not yours, but God's" (2 Chron. 20:15). He then described the precise route the invaders would take in approaching Jerusalem. Furthermore, he declared, "You will not need to fight in this battle. Position yourselves, stand still and see the salvation of the LORD, who is with you, O Judah and Jerusalem! Do not fear or be dismayed; tomorrow go out against them, for the LORD is with you" (2 Chron. 20:17).

How could a choir of praisers with a promise be taken out by a host of invaders?

What a promise! And my, how it infused Jehoshaphat with confidence! That promise put such boldness in Jehoshaphat's soul that he decided to throw all caution to the wind. Yes, it's true that he mobilized his army; but instead of sending the army out first, he placed his praise choir in the front. So the first ones to march toward the enemy lines were singers who praised God's holiness, saying, "Praise the LORD, for His mercy endures forever" (2 Chron. 20:21).

It seems that Jehoshaphat was thinking along these lines, "Since God has promised to fight this battle, and since He has said that we don't need to fight, there is no need to send the armies out first. Why not just give thanks and praise to God for the glory of His promise and goodness to us?"

Talk about audacity! Placing your weaponless choir on the front lines of the battle—that's brash! Bold! Preposterous!

"What happened?" someone might ask. Well, when the choir began to sing and praise the Lord, God sent ambushments of angels against the invading armies, and they turned on one another and destroyed one another. By the time it was done, they had all killed one another and no one had escaped. All the people of Judah had to do was carry away the plunder—a three-day job.

Let me ask you a question. How could a choir of praisers with a promise be taken out by a host of invaders? Not possible.

PETER

Peter had been promised by Jesus that he would live to an old age (John 21:18). Around twelve to fifteen years later, Peter was imprisoned by Herod (Acts 12:3), who intended to kill him. At the time, Peter was still a relatively young man, however, and he had that promise from Jesus that he would live to be an old man. How does a middle-aged man with a promise like that respond to this kind of imprisonment? The text tells us.

The night before Peter's slated trial and execution, he lay fast asleep in his cell, chained between two guards. Why stay up and worry about tomorrow's execution when you're living under the shelter of an unfulfilled promise? That promise put such confidence in Peter's soul that he happily fell into a deep and refreshing sleep on the eve of his seemingly inescapable death.

What happened? Well, an angel came to Peter's cell, woke him up with a solid thump, released him from his chains, and led him out of the prison. The main gate of the prison opened of its own accord and Peter walked out a free man.

Little wonder, later in life, that Peter would describe God's promises as "exceedingly great and precious"

(2 Pet. 1:4). He had experienced the preserving power of an unfulfilled promise.

Let me ask a question. How could a man who has a promise from the lips of the Master Himself possibly suffer a premature death at the hands of a megalomaniac? Not possible.

How could a man with a promise possibly suffer a premature death at the hands of a megalomaniac?

The lives of Abraham, Caleb, David, Jehoshaphat, and Peter exemplify how promise produces boldness. Do you also hold a divine promise? Then let it infuse your soul with the bold assurance that God is going to deliver on His promise.

Okay, so you haven't received your breakthrough yet. Okay, so all you have is a promise. But do you know what you've got?

AUDACITY

Thanks for letting me chase that trail in chapter six on boldness. Now, let's return to our parable, and specifically, verse 8.

> "I say to you, though he will not rise and give to him because he is his friend, yet because of his persistence he will rise and give him as many as he needs" (Luke 11:8).

First of all, I want to comment on the phrase, "though he will not rise and give to him because he is his friend." Jesus indicated that Dave's friendship with Jim was not enough to spur him to pull himself out of bed. The friendship was strong and enduring, but honoring the friendship alone wasn't enough motivation for Dave to disrupt his entire household.

Sometimes friendship with God, in itself, is not enough.

When God postpones the answer to your prayer, it can be tempting to question the legitimacy of your intimacy with God. "God, what kind of a friendship do we have, anyways? I thought our intimacy was meaningful, and our history together strong. But You're not answering my prayer. Am I delusional? Is our friendship not as strong as I've thought?"

Based upon our parable, I hear the Lord answering, "I love the intimacy that you and I enjoy. The issue here isn't friendship; the issue is disruption."

If relationship were the sole factor, Jim, you'd already have your three loaves. But the disruption factor is very strong. If you're going to get bread, Jim, you'll have to be persistent.

There's some stuff that intimacy alone won't get you. Some stuff requires persistence.

There's some stuff that intimacy alone won't get you. Some stuff requires persistence.

And now we have come to the second colorful word in our parable. *Persistence.*

PERSISTENCE

Persistence is the way the New King James Version translates the original Greek word, *anaideia*. *Anaideia* is a compound word, meaning it is two Greek words joined together to form a new word. It is composed of the word *an*, which means "no," and the word *aidos*, which means "shame." *No shame*. The most literal English equivalent would probably be *shamelessness*.

Among English translations, the most common rendering by translators of *anaideia* is either *persistence* or *importunity*. But *persistence* falls short of identifying *anaideia*.

Importunity comes a bit closer. Importunity is defined as, "the fact of being troublesomely demanding or insistent; a demand made repeatedly or insistently."[1] *Importunity* is close, but I submit that *anaideia* demands

1 Encarta® World English Dictionary © 1999 Microsoft Corporation.

an even closer translation.

Since *shamelessness* (Darby's rendering) is a rather awkward word in English, arguably the best English translation for *anaideia* is *audacity*. "Yet because of his *audacity* he will rise and give him as many as he needs."

Anaideia is not pointing to the fact that Jim is knocking on Dave's door without stopping; it's pointing to the fact that he's doing it at midnight. It's not describing his repetitive knocking, but rather the relational rudeness of doing it at such an unreasonable hour. It's describing the impropriety of Jim's behavior at midnight.

Anaideia is labeling Jim's behavior as impudence, impoliteness, effrontery, nerve, or brash boldness. *Anaideia* is an absence of decorum. Invasiveness. Unapologetic rudeness, to the point of being relationally reckless.

Because of his *anaideia*, Jim is actually hazarding his relationship with Dave. He is going to find out if his friendship with Dave is strong enough to bear up under such strain, or whether it will break.

Look at how Jesus is teaching us to pray! We are to come to God with the relational confidence that we can be shameless and audacious in our demands, and trust that our friendship with Him is strong enough to sustain the strain.

What good is a relationship with God if you can't lean on it in your time of need?

"You have a friendship with God," Jesus is saying. "Lean on it. Put pressure on the relationship."

What good is a relationship with God if you can't lean on it in your time of need?

Ah, my friend, when you have built a friendship with

God over time, you gain confidence to pray with audacity. Relationship makes you bold.

ASKING FOR ANOTHER

One reason Jim is so bold to stand at Dave's door at midnight and ask for bread is because he isn't asking for himself. This isn't a myopic, self-serving request; this is Jim asking for bread so he can serve another.

Jim wasn't irresponsible in his planning. He had no idea Chris would suddenly show up and request to spend the night. Circumstances were beyond his control, so Jim was shameless. He needed bread for his guest.

When you're asking Jesus for divine bread so that you have something to give to your needy friends, it gives you the confidence to pray with audacity. You're fighting for a cause bigger than just your own appetites. "This isn't just for me, Jesus. It's for them. So give me Your healing bread."

YIDDISH

A certain English translation, called the *Complete Jewish Bible*, has been written especially for Jewish readers. It's a translation that sometimes uses Hebrew, Aramaic, or Yiddish words to help Jewish readers understand and connect with the text.

To translate *anaideia* in Luke 11:8, the *Complete Jewish Bible* does not say *persistence*, but rather uses the word *chutzpah* (or alternatively, *hutzpah*). Here's the verse as it appears in the CJB:

> But I tell you, even if he won't get up because the man is his friend, yet because of the man's *hutzpah* he will get up and give him as much as he needs.

Yiddish is a language that originated in central Europe in the ninth century and is based on the Hebrew language but incorporates many German words. *Chutzpah* came to us originally as a Yiddish word.

In its Glossary, the *Complete Jewish Bible* defines *chutzpah* as "boldness, audacity, insolence, nerve, gall."

For even fuller clarity, let's go to Leo Rosten's book, *The Joys of Yiddish*, in which he defines *chutzpah* as "gall, brazen nerve, effrontery, incredible 'guts,' presumption plus arrogance such as no other word and no other language can do justice to."

Chutzpah: Gall, brazen nerve, effrontery, incredible "guts," presumption plus arrogance such as no other word and no other language can do justice to.

Rosten is telling us *chutzpah* is such a deeply colorful and thoroughly Jewish word that it has no equivalent in any other language. Apparently we agreed with him because the English language took the Yiddish word and just placed it, as is, into the English dictionary. So now chutzpah is an English word, and its meaning is identical to the Yiddish.

It's derived from the Hebrew word *hutspa*. *Hutspa* does not occur in the Hebrew Old Testament, but it is in the Hebrew lexicon. When translated into English, *hutspa* means *insolence* or *audacity*. In fact, in conversational Hebrew *hutspa* is most commonly viewed as a negative quality because of the rudeness factor. It's usually not a complimentary word.

HEBREW OR ARAMAIC?

In a moment I want us to look at Luke 11:8 in Franz Delitzsch's, *"The Delitzsch Hebrew Gospels."* But first I want to explain why that volume was written.

Franz Delitzsch is an internationally acclaimed authority on Semitic languages. He is probably best known for co-authoring the epic *Keil and Delitzsch Commentary on the Old Testament*—a prodigious ten-volume commentary that mines the Hebrew text of the Old Testament.

Delitzsch has weighed in on one of the more controversial questions of Jesus' ministry, namely this: Which language did Jesus speak when He taught the masses on the hills of Galilee? Scholars have struggled for centuries with this question. When I was a Bible School student in 1980, I was told that Jesus taught in Aramaic. Aramaic is primarily a Syrian language that the Jews would have learned during their captivity in Babylon. Laban spoke Aramaic (Gen. 31:47), and it's a prominent language in the Jewish Talmud. It would have been brought to Israel by the exiles who returned from Babylon. It was spoken widely in the time of Jesus, and since my instructors were so confident, I believed them when they asserted that Jesus taught in Aramaic.

But since then, I have come to discover that the Aramaic question is far from settled. Because of recent research, a growing body of scholarship is declaring unapologetically that Jesus taught in Hebrew. Go ahead and do a simple online search, you'll probably agree that the arguments for Hebrew are quite compelling. The growing body of evidence indicates that Jesus taught the masses of His day in Hebrew.

Delitzsch favors this view. Given his credentials in

understanding Semitic languages, it is significant that he insists the fabric of the New Testament Greek points back, not to an Aramaic origin, but to a Hebrew origination. Said another way, Delitzsch is persuaded that when Matthew, Mark, Luke, and John translated Jesus' words into Greek (for all four Gospels are written in Greek), they were translating words spoken initially in Hebrew, not Aramaic.

Delitzsch felt so strongly about this that he decided to write an entire volume based on this premise. I am referring now to his work, *The Delitzsch Hebrew Gospels*. Delitzsch sat down with the Greek text as it appears in the four Gospels, and began to ask himself, "If Jesus taught in Hebrew, what were His actual, original words? If the Gospel writers translated His Hebrew words into Greek, what were the Hebrew words originally upon His lips?" So Delitzsch began to write a "backwards" translation. Since the Gospels were translated from Hebrew into Greek, he decided to translate the Greek of the Gospels "back" into Hebrew. His goal was to represent, as accurately as possible, the actual Hebrew words that would have been on the Master's lips as He taught His disciples.

In *The Delitzsch Hebrew Gospels*, when Delitzsch translated Luke 11:8, and came upon the Greek word *anaideia*, can you suppose what Hebrew word he said *anaideia* was pointing back to? You guessed it. The Hebrew word, *hutspa*.

Delitzsch is claiming that the actual word on the lips of Christ, when He delivered this parable, was the word *hutspa*. "Yet because of his *hutspa* he will rise and give him as many as he needs."

Then, where *hutspa* occurs in Luke 11:8, Delitzsch

has an asterisk. At the bottom of the page he gives a literal rendering of *hutspa*: "strong-faced-ness."

Strong-faced-ness!

"On account of strong-faced-ness he will get up and give to him everything he needs."

What a delightfully compelling word! Jesus is teaching us how to push back. He is coaching us to challenge the sovereignty of God's timing with strong-faced-ness.

Bartimaeus, you want Jesus to touch your eyes and heal you. But if you succumb to the pressure of the people crowding around you, and just offer sophisticated, cultured prayers, you'll probably stay blind. To get your healing, you're going to have to defy the crowd that wants you to be quiet and composed. You're going to have to push back with strong-faced-ness and lift your voice in a desperate cry (Mark 10:46).

The Syro-Phoenician woman wanted Jesus to deliver her daughter from a tormenting demon (Mark 7:26). Had she succumbed to intimidation and limited herself to dignified, elegant prayers, she wouldn't have gotten very far. She had to push back against Jesus with chutzpah in order to get her answer.

Maybe you have time for safe, polite prayers. B u t I don't. The hour is too late and our world too desperate for polished prayers. We need revival *now*. We need prayers with strong-faced-ness.

Misty Edwards once asked, "How do you hurry Someone from eternity?" I know only one way. Chutzpah.

CHUTZPAH!

Since the evidence indicates that Jesus actually used the Hebrew word *hutspa* when He delivered our parable, let's change *persistence* (as the New King James Version renders it) to our English/Yiddish word *chutzpah* and allow the reading of the verse to be as follows:

> "I say to you, though he will not rise and give to him because he is his friend, yet because of his chutzpah he will rise and give him as many as he needs" (Luke 11:8).

Jesus is beckoning us to "strong-faced-ness" in prayer!

This is John Knox praying, "Give me Scotland or I die."

"Fill me or kill me."

"Answer me, or take me home."

I once heard Mark Batterson say that God honors bold prayers because bold prayers honor God.

But again, we pray with chutzpah because of our intimacy with God. Chutzpah without relationship can backfire on you. That's what happened, for example, when the elders of Israel chose to bring the ark of the covenant into their war with the Philistines (see 1 Samuel 4). The nation was backslidden and far from God, and even though they demonstrated chutzpah in bringing the ark to the battleground, it didn't work. The ark was actually captured by the Philistines and Israel suffered a dreadful defeat.

Audacity *without* relationship is presumption. Audacity *because of* relationship can change world history.

Audacity without relationship is presumption. Audacity because of relationship can change world history.

When I think of how chutzpah will make bold demands of God, I am reminded of a conversation Jesus had with Martha. To look at the conversation, we need to return to the story of the raising of Lazarus.

While Jesus was in another part of Israel with His disciples, His friend Lazarus took sick and died. The family sent for Jesus and, after delaying a couple days, Jesus headed for His friends' place in Bethany. By the time He finally arrived, Lazarus had already been dead four days.

Upon his arrival, Martha went out to meet Him. In her distress over her brother's death, she said to Him, "Lord, if You had been here, my brother would not have died" (John 11:20). She knew that if Jesus had gotten to Lazarus before he had died, he would have been healed. By implication, it's clear she was distraught over Jesus' late arrival.

In reply, Jesus said to her, "Your brother will rise again" (John 11:23).

Now, that statement could be taken in at least two ways. The most demanding sense of the statement would mean, "Your brother will rise again *now*." The softer sense of the statement would mean, "Your brother will rise again in the final resurrection."

Martha wanted to be easy on Jesus. She didn't want to place undue pressure on Him. So she took His words in their softest, most metaphorical or mystical sense, and gave Jesus an "easy out" by replying, "I know that he will rise again in the resurrection at the last day" (John 11:24).

In my natural understanding, I think it was sweet of Martha to release Jesus from the burden of having to pull off an immediate, literal, bodily resurrection. But Jesus didn't seem to think Martha was doing Him any favors.

I want you to look carefully at how Jesus responded to Martha. There's something here for us to learn. He basically said to her, "Martha, you're interpreting My words in their least demanding sense, but I'm wanting you to interpret them in their most demanding sense. What is the most difficult, immediate way for My words to be fulfilled?"

That's my interpretation of Jesus' meaning. Here are His actual words: "I am the resurrection and the life. He who believes in Me, though he may die, he shall live. And whoever lives and believes in Me shall never die. Do you believe this?" (John 11:25-26). Jesus was implying, "Martha, you think you're being nice to Me by applying My words to the resurrection at the end of the age. But you have the resurrection and the life standing before you in the flesh. Resurrection is as easy for Me right now as it will be in the last day. When I say that your brother will rise again, I mean exactly that. I have come to raise him from the dead."

To prove His intent, Jesus then proceeded to the tomb and resurrected Lazarus.

Here's the compelling principle we learn from this

story: Jesus wants us to take His word in its most immediate, demanding sense. When He gives you a promise, what's the most demanding way for that promise to be fulfilled? Raise the bar of your expectations, and insist on a fulfillment that requires the most power.

Jesus wants us to take His word in its most immediate, demanding sense.

He says to you, "I am the Lord who heals you." The soft reading says, "I am the Lord who heals some of you, some of the time. And if you're not healed in this life, you'll be healed in the next." The most demanding reading says, "I am the Lord who heals you now, in this life. Supernaturally. All by Myself. Every time."

He wants you to understand His promises to mean what they say. You're doing Him no favors by mystifying, symbolizing, or allegorizing them.

What is harder for God to do—to raise you up now, or raise you up in the last day? To heal you now, or heal you in the resurrection? Both are equally easy to our God for whom nothing is impossible. No more dumbing down His promises and symbolically applying them to some far-off fulfillment. Because He doesn't call it a favor, He calls it unbelief.

Always take God's word in its most demanding, immediate, face-value sense. If you do, you will pray with chutzpah. "Jesus, You said it, and I'm taking You at Your word. Give me Your promise! Now!"

CHUTZPAH STORIES

When I think of prayers with chutzpah, my mind goes back to stories I've read about Smith Wigglesworth, an evangelist who ministered in the first half of the twentieth century. I'll tell a couple of my favorites very briefly.[1]

In one of his healing crusades, a man with cancer in his abdominal area was wheeled into the meeting on a hospital stretcher. He was on his death bed and could barely move. A doctor stood attentively at his side, monitoring his condition. Wigglesworth made his way down the aisle. When he got to the man laying lifelessly on the bed, he asked what was wrong with him. He was told the man had cancer in his stomach. Wigglesworth clenched his fist, drew his arm back, and punched the man directly in the stomach. (For Wigglesworth, he saw cancer as demonic, so he was striking at the demonic source.) The man let out a cry, his arms fell down, and he appeared to die. The doctor began to scream, "He's dead! He's dead!" Looking at Wigglesworth, he said, "You've killed him! The family will sue you!"

Wigglesworth calmly looked at the doctor and said, "He's healed." Then he proceeded to keep walking down the aisle, moving on to the next person.

About ten minutes later, the man came onto the platform. He had gotten out of his bed, moved his doctor aside, and was walking around in his hospital gown with his back side peeking out. But he didn't care. With his arms lifted high, he was screaming, "I'm healed! I'm healed!" By then the doctor had gotten on board and was behind him, yelling, "He's healed! He's healed!"

The man was healed because of a hard punch to the gut. Where is *that* in the Bible? You can't minister divine healing by punching people in their cancer. That's illegal.

Chutzpah.

1 Lester Sumrall, *Pioneers of Faith*, Tulsa, OK: Harrison House, 1995, pp. 172-175.

One more Wigglesworth story. Smith was ministering in a church in Australia, and his host took him to a fancy restaurant for a Sunday lunch. Only wealthy people ate there. Looking around the restaurant, he noticed that virtually none of the patrons were visibly praying over their meal before eating. So he stood up at his table, took his water glass and fork in hand, and began to clang noisily on the glass. Everyone in the restaurant immediately hushed, stopped eating, and turned. He lifted his voice and said something to the following effect, "Ladies and gentlemen, I noticed since arriving here that none of you prayed over your food. You resemble a bunch of hogs to me. You just jump in and eat without giving thanks to the One who provided it for you. Bow your heads, and I'll pray for you." And with that announcement he raised his hands, prayed for the people, offered thanks to God for everyone's meal, and then sat down.

His host pastor said that before they left the place, two families made their way over to Wigglesworth and confessed that a spirit of conviction came upon them during his prayer. Right there in the restaurant they gave their lives to Christ. I'm not sure it's legal to call people a bunch of hogs and then lead them in prayer, but it produced eternal fruit.

Speaking of restaurant stories, Bill Johnson told the story of a guy who stood on his chair in a restaurant, lifted his voice for all the patrons to hear, and called out, "I'm in love with a Man!" Immediately, he had the attention of the entire room. He witnessed to Christ, and some people in the restaurant gave their lives to Christ that day.

Chutzpah.

A BLIND EYE IS OPENED

Let me tell a more recent story from my friend, Shane Warren, who is a pastor in West Monroe, Louisiana. During a TV interview with Sid Roth,[2] he told of the time he took a group of student interns from his school of ministry to some meetings in Mississippi. In the middle of the meeting, Shane felt like the Lord interrupted him and told him to pray for the sick.

When Shane offered the call for prayer ministry, a woman came forward who was blind in one eye. The eye was white and milky, looking almost as though it didn't even have a pupil at all. In that moment, faith sprang up in Shane's heart, and as he said in his own words, "I knew that I knew that I knew this woman was getting ready to get her sight in that eye."

With this confidence filling his heart, Shane called all the students forward. He had them stand in the front with him so that, as this woman faced him, they had a direct view of her face. He said to them, "I want to show you the power of God." Shane wanted the students to see a demonstration of the power of God before their very eyes.

If Shane had called the students forward *after* the woman had been healed, that would have been understandable. But to call them forward *before* the woman is healed? And to announce that they are about to see the power of God? That kind of public declaration requires bold faith—the kind of faith that comes from God alone. You can exercise this kind of chutzpah only when you have received a download of faith from the Holy Spirit.

2 http://sidroth.org/television/tv-archives/shane-warren

Then the Lord gave Shane the specific words to pray. Sensing the Lord's direction, Shane said, "Eyes, look straight on." As soon as he spoke those words, it was like a milky substance began to dissolve from her eye, and they watched as a pupil formed clearly and quickly in that eye.

Several of the students started stepping backwards, and calling out, "Oh my, oh my." The woman began to scream, "I can see! I can see!" The entire congregation began to rejoice, and in response several people gave their lives to Christ.

God did a miracle as Shane stepped out in faith and prayed with chutzpah.

GOD OPENS A DOOR IN ASIA

My friend, Mark (not his real name), leads a ministry that plants churches in a remote region of Asia that restricts access for Christians. Mark told me about the time he and a team of medical professionals were in a certain hostile area, demonstrating Christ's love through medical help.

Some of the local children were susceptible to a certain malady specific to that particular region. When children were diagnosed to have this malady, surgery would be performed, extending their life expectancy and improving their quality of life. During the entire process, blessings would be quietly prayed over each child, and opportunities would be sought to witness for Christ to the families involved.

Mark knew, because of previous trips, that every move of the team would be hawkishly scrutinized. In that region, there were many enemies of the gospel among the community leaders. Perhaps that's why, prior to the trip, the Lord clearly led Mark to alert hundreds of intercessors via email, asking them to consider fasting and praying for protection and favor as the team departed for this risky operation. The Lord spoke to Mark from Esther 4:13-16, where it says, "Go...gather... fast."

Upon arrival, the team could feel the tension in the air, but they moved forward in faith. The first day, they examined literally hundreds of children at a large elementary school. Everything went smoothly. The local officials were favorable to them, the school teachers were at ease, and the children were happy. The team even taught the children some songs with a gentle gospel message. Their strategy for reaching this remote people group was working.

But something happened overnight. The officials' hearts were suddenly hardened, almost inexplicably, and when the team returned to the school the next day to continue their work, they found the doors shut. Faces were dark, and those who were supposed to be their hosts now spewed threats.

Mark quickly sent a text to his wife, asking her to mobilize their prayer partners around the world. Then he gathered his team on the grounds of the schoolyard where their equipment sat in a pile. From all four floors of the schoolhouse, hundreds of eyes stared in bewilderment from the classroom windows. Mark and the team felt exposed and on display. A moment of truth had come.

Mark called on his team to pray, saying, "Beloved, we serve a great and powerful God. Before leaving for this trip, He prepared me with the picture of Esther who called on the Jews to go, gather, and fast. At this very moment, the call to intercede has gone forth around the world. God is surely on our side, and if He is for us, who can be against us?"

The team joined hands in faith-filled prayer, and then that's when things began to get bold. Right then and there, in the school courtyard, they began to sing. They lifted their voices and sang out the praises of God. The ears of all those children, as well as the persecuting officials, heard a sound such as they had never heard before. Who knows what they were thinking? But the song grew in strength and arose from that courtyard to the Maker of heaven and earth—a song that confronted the powers of darkness that had reigned in the region for centuries. They lifted their voices to Him who holds all peoples, all history, and even the future in His hands.

Suddenly, Mark felt they needed to make a move. All those eyes followed them as they picked up the heavy medical equipment and walked from the playground toward the school gate. Where were they to go? Mark had no clue! He just knew they had to move decisively. Quickly, they approached the gate.

When they walked out of the school gate, at that very moment a van pulled up and stopped right in front of them. A man stepped out, reached out his hand, and said, "Please come with me. We've prepared another school for you to go to."

Without losing a step, they loaded their equipment into the van and then followed the van on foot to another school that was in close proximity. Over the next two days, they were able to assess hundreds of children in a kindergarten. Three of those children had serious conditions which required life-saving surgery. The surgeries were performed, the families were shown care, and the team marvelled as hearts melted towards the Lord. Children's lives were saved and, even better, souls were saved. God had responded to the audacious prayers and bold praises of His people.

GOD OPENS A DOOR IN EUROPE

My friends, Dale and Cheryl Anderson, served as missionaries to Poland for seven years during the 1990s. For the first five years, they lived with other people in their apartments, which had positive aspects to it, but never gave them a sense of having their own home.

After five years of that, a deep longing grew in Cheryl's heart for an apartment of their own. But they were poor missionaries living on a meager salary and they simply could not afford their own place. Cheryl felt stuck between an insatiable longing for their own home and the reality of having no financial resources.

When she spoke with her friends about this desire, she was told to be satisfied with what God had given. Her friends were irritated when she began to look around at flats for purchase, but there was a glimmer of hope in Cheryl's soul and she would not be deterred from her search. And yet, she fought anxiety and fear as she struggled with the common sense of her friends. Cheryl told me, "I was so stressed that at times I went from tree to tree and vomited."

One night, she and Dale committed the situation to the Lord in prayer, putting it in His hands. The next morning, they both awoke with a price in mind. This gave them the confidence that God was speaking and providing direction. This price meant that Cheryl could start to search for nicer apartments in a higher price range.

Their friends seemed to grow increasingly frustrated during this time because Cheryl would not settle for their advice. They thought Cheryl should be searching for something more frugal.

One day she found an apartment that seemed perfect. It was large enough for them and their children, located in the center of town, and it had a balcony overlooking an enclosed flower garden. Just lovely! And the cost was much more than they could afford.

During this time, a man from the Netherlands came to their town. He and Cheryl had a lengthy visit one evening, and their conversation included talk about real estate. She told him about the apartment she had looked at, and he asked how they would pay for it.

At first, Cheryl hesitated. Then a boldness took hold of her. She opened her mouth and declared, "If God can give me this growing confidence and lead me to the apartment, then He has a plan." Hearing those words come out of her mouth even strengthened her own soul!

After returning to the Netherlands, this man called them and said, "Before I left Poland, the Lord spoke to me and said that I am to pay for your apartment." Once again Cheryl got bold and asked, "Are you going to follow through with that?" He paused, and then said, "Yes. Yes, I am."

The Dutchman fulfilled his commitment and paid cash for the house, giving it outright to Dale and Cheryl. And the Anderson's delighted in the goodness of the Lord to give them such a wonderful place of their own.

I'm including their story here because I love how God honored the bold prayers and proclamations of a mother who longed to have a home for her family. Truly

God cares about all the things that concern us. And He responds to chutzpah.

A HEARING OR A HANGING

To summarize the parable we've been examining, Jim needs Dave's three loaves of bread so he can feed his out-of-town guest who showed up unexpectedly at midnight. Dave doesn't want to arise for Jim because he doesn't want to awaken his family. Jim pushes back insistently because he doesn't need bread in the morning, he needs bread *now*. By standing at Dave's door at midnight contrary to Dave's wishes, Jim is actually breaking the law. But it's Jim's audacity that causes Dave to finally get out of bed and give him the bread he needs.

Jesus was teaching us to pray like Jim—with chutzpah—because we have such a strong, confident friendship with God. The parable ends with Jim getting everything he needs, which serves to show how strongly Jesus wants us to obtain answers to prayer. As Jesus said at the close of the parable:

> "So I say to you, ask, and it will be given to you; seek, and you will find; knock, and it will be opened to you. For everyone who asks receives, and he who seeks finds, and to him who knocks it will be opened" (Luke 11:5-10).

Based on this parable, here's the message of this book in a nutshell: Contend for answered prayer! Break the rules and pray illegal prayers! When God says, "Not yet," push back on His providential timing with chutzpah! Pray bold, epochal prayers that change the times and seasons in which we live!

Bill and Jen, mentioned in chapter two for their fight with cancer, realized that they must pray with chutzpah if they are to receive *now* what God was intending to do *tomorrow*.

In closing, please look at one final example in the Bible of illegal prayers. May this story strengthen your heart to be courageously audacious in prayer. Our final story is taken from the book of Esther.

ESTHER GOES ILLEGAL

Under Haman's evil incitement, the king of Persia passed a law that all the Jews in the empire were to be killed on a certain day.

When Mordecai read the decree to destroy the Jews, he sent a copy of the decree to his cousin, Esther, who had become queen because of her outstanding beauty. He told her that she should go to the king and plead to him on behalf of her people.

In her reply to Mordecai, Esther noted the dangerous nature of coming before the king uninvited. (Notice below that the phrases in the story I want to emphasize are capitalized.) She said,

> All the king's servants and the people of the king's provinces know that any man or woman who goes into the INNER COURT to the king, who has not been called, he has but one law: put all to death, except the one to whom the king holds out the golden scepter, that he may live (Est. 4:11).

Mordecai realized he was commanding Esther to do something dangerous, but the lives of thousands of Jews were at stake. So he responded to Esther in this manner:

> Do not think in your heart that you will escape in the king's palace any more than all the other Jews. For if you remain completely silent at this time, relief and deliverance will arise for the Jews from another place, but you and your father's house will perish. Yet who knows whether you have come to the kingdom for such a time as this? (Est. 4:13-14).

Esther honored and loved Mordecai, who had raised her in his home, so she acquiesced with this reply:

> Go, gather all the Jews who are present in Shushan, and fast for me; neither eat nor drink for three days, night or day. My maids and I will fast likewise. And so I will go to the king, WHICH IS AGAINST THE LAW; and if I perish, I perish! (Est. 4:15-16).

It was against the law to step, uninvited, into the inner court, which I will explain more fully in a moment.

The next chapter tells the story of Esther's coming before the king. You'll notice that she put on her best outfit for this mission because, when you're doing something illegal and bold, you want to look especially beautiful to the king.

> Now it happened on the third day that Esther put on her royal robes and stood in the INNER COURT of the king's palace, across from the king's house, while the king sat on his royal throne in the royal house, facing the entrance of the house. So it was, when the king saw Queen Esther standing in the court, that she found favor in his sight, and the king held out to Esther the

> golden scepter that was in his hand. Then Esther went near and touched the top of the scepter. And the king said to her, "What do you wish, Queen Esther? What is your request? It shall be given to you—up to half the kingdom!" (Est. 5:1-3).

The king realized that Esther, by standing in the inner court, was putting her life on the line. He was probably wondering to himself, *What request is so important to you, that you're willing to risk everything in order to present it to me?* Rather than being put off by her boldness, he wanted to know more.

Esther presented herself to the king by going illegal and standing, uninvited, in the inner court. As a result, she got a hearing and was able to present her petition.

All of this is to be contrasted with what happened to Haman in the following chapter. Here's the story as the Bible records it.

> That night the king could not sleep. So one was commanded to bring the book of the records of the chronicles; and they were read before the king. And it was found written that Mordecai had told of Bigthana and Teresh, two of the king's eunuchs, the doorkeepers who had sought to lay hands on King Ahasuerus. Then the king said, "What honor or dignity has been bestowed on Mordecai for this?" And the king's servants who attended him said, "Nothing has been done for him." So the king said, "Who is in the court?" Now Haman had just entered the OUTER COURT of the king's palace to suggest that the king hang Mordecai on the gallows that he had prepared for him. The king's servants said to him, "Haman is there, standing in the court." And the king said, "Let him come in." So Haman came in, and the king asked him, "What shall be done for the man whom the king delights to honor?" Now Haman thought in his

> heart, "Whom would the king delight to honor more than me?" And Haman answered the king, "For the man whom the king delights to honor, let a royal robe be brought which the king has worn, and a horse on which the king has ridden, which has a royal crest placed on its head. Then let this robe and horse be delivered to the hand of one of the king's most noble princes, that he may array the man whom the king delights to honor. Then parade him on horseback through the city square, and proclaim before him: 'Thus shall it be done to the man whom the king delights to honor!'" Then the king said to Haman, "Hurry, take the robe and the horse, as you have suggested, and do so for Mordecai the Jew who sits within the king's gate! Leave nothing undone of all that you have spoken"(Est. 6:1-10).

I have capitalized the words INNER COURT and OUTER COURT in the above passages because I want to emphasize the distinction between them. The king of Persia had two courts in his palace—an outer court, and an inner court. The law specified that if anyone had a petition to make of the king, they were to come to the outer court, take a number, be seated, and wait their turn. Once the king called for them, they were escorted to the inner court where they stood before the king and presented their case.

It was against the law to step directly into the inner court, an offense punishable by death. The purpose of the law was to protect the king from assassination attempts or harm. There was a prescribed way to approach the king, and it involved coming to the outer court and waiting to be summoned.

Esther went directly into the inner court, contrary to the law, because her life was on the line. She was about to reveal to the king that she was a Jew. If the king would refuse to overturn the decree to kill the Jews, Esther would be killed anyways. So she decided that if she was going to reveal her Jewish identity, she may as well go for broke and step into the inner court. It was all or nothing. Desperation drove her to break the law.

By not loving her life, even unto death, she actually saved it.

In Haman's case, he really hated Mordecai, and that's why he came to the king. He wanted permission to hang Mordecai on his newly-constructed gallows. But he wasn't as desperate as Esther. He didn't hate Mordecai so much that he was willing to put his life on the line. Haman had too much to lose to step directly into the inner court. He loved his life too much to gamble with it. That's why he chose the safe way, the legal way, the way of self-preservation. He decided to pray legal prayers. So he went to the outer court, took a number, sat down, and waited to be called by the king into the inner court.

What might have happened if Haman had brought his petition into the inner court, against the law? I think there's a chance the king would have received him, and would have asked him, "What in the world do you desire this badly?" But as it turned out, the king never even got around to the question. Haman lacked the courage to pray illegal prayers, and consequently was not even given the opportunity to verbalize his request. By playing it safe, he suffered shipwreck. Wanting to save his life, he lost it.

Haman prayed legal prayers and didn't even get a hearing; Esther prayed illegal prayers and got a hearing with the king.

Haman prayed legal prayers and didn't even get a

hearing; Esther prayed illegal prayers and got a hearing with the king.

If Esther steps into the inner court and gets a hearing, we call her bold. If she steps into the inner court and gets a hanging, we call her presumptuous. Sometimes, there's a fine line between boldness and presumption.

Haman loved his life, and lost it. Esther lost her life, and saved it

In the king's palatial sprawl, there was a bedchamber, and there was a throneroom. They were not the same room. Had Esther desired intimacy, she might have gone to the bedchamber. But that's not what she was after; she wanted justice. She wanted the king to pass legislation on her behalf. So she went to the throneroom—the inner court.

The book of Esther is the story of two queens who broke the law. Vashti broke the law by pulling away from the king (Est. 1:10-12). Esther broke the law by drawing near to the king (Est. 5:2). If you're going to pray illegal prayers, get close. Draw near to God.

If you're going to pray illegal prayers, get close.

SERVING THE KING AN ULTIMATUM

When Esther entered the inner court, she didn't say a word. She simply stood and looked pretty. Just by standing there, she was serving the king an ultimatum. "Give me a hearing, or give me a hanging."

Now, not just any old scallywag could gain entrance to the inner court. It was carefully guarded. If a madman came along and tried to forcibly enter the inner court, he'd be stopped by the guards and executed ever before he made it into the inner court. Getting access to the inner court was a feat all its own.

How did Queen Esther gain access to the inner court? We're not told. So the following conversation is imagined; it's my best attempt to conceive how she gained access to the inner court.

Esther came to the outer court, approached the entrance to the inner court, and said, "Open the door."

The guard at the door respectfully replied, "I'm sorry, my Lady, but I can't do that."

"Open the door."

"You're not allowed in there, my Lady."

"Open the door."

"Take a seat here in the outer court, my Lady. I'll tell the king you want to speak with him."

"Open the door."

"Please, my Lady, be nice. Take a seat in the outer court. I know the king will be eager to invite you in."

"Open the door!"

"But you could hang on the gallows for this!"

"I know. Open the door."

"Yes, my Lady."

And the guard opened the door so that Queen Esther could step into the inner court and pray illegal prayers. Only someone with vested relationship could get into that inner court uninvited.

Once confronted by Esther's presence, the king had to make a decision. He could not stall or delay his response. Forced in that moment to banish or receive her, he raised his scepter, invited her to draw near, and inquired into her petition. He was favorable to her because of the intimacy of their relationship.

We're after the same thing Esther was after. We want

to enter the inner court, which Charles Price called "the garden of answered prayer," and have an audience with the King. It's the holy pursuit of the noble soul. And we're willing to lay our lives on the line in order to get there.

If I am reading the book of Esther correctly, it seems to me that somewhere, in the courts of the King, there is an inner court where, if you can just get there, you can serve Him an ultimatum. "Give me a hearing, or give me a hanging."

"Answer me, or kill me."

Someone might complain, "But isn't that kind of prayer illegal?"

Exactly.

ALL OF BOB SORGE'S TITLES

ILLEGAL PRAYERS $10

A COVENANT WITH MY EYES $13

EXPLORING WORSHIP:

A Practical Guide to Praise & Worship $16

Exploring Worship WORKBOOK & DISCUSSION GUIDE .... $ 5

IN HIS FACE: A Prophetic Call to Renewed Focus $13

THE FIRE OF DELAYED ANSWERS $14

THE FIRE OF GOD'S LOVE $13

PAIN, PERPLEXITY, AND PROMOTION:

A Prophetic Interpretation of the Book of Job $14

DEALING WITH THE REJECTION AND PRAISE OF MAN $10

GLORY: When Heaven Invades Earth $10

SECRETS OF THE SECRET PLACE $15

Secrets of the Secret Place: COMPANION STUDY GUIDE $11

Secrets of the Secret Place: LEADER'S MANUAL .... $ 5

ENVY: The Enemy Within $12

FOLLOWING THE RIVER: A Vision for Corporate Worship $10

LOYALTY: The Reach of the Noble Heart $14

UNRELENTING PRAYER $13

POWER OF THE BLOOD: Approaching God with Confidence $13

IT'S NOT BUSINESS, IT'S PERSONAL $10

OPENED FROM THE INSIDE: Taking the Stronghold of Zion $11

MINUTE MEDITATIONS $12

BETWEEN THE LINES: God is Writing Your Story $13

DVD Series:

EXPLORING WORSHIP DVD SERIES $30

SECRETS OF THE SECRET PLACE DVD SERIES $30

To order Bob's materials:

- Go to www.oasishouse.com
- Call 816-767-8880 (ask about quantity discounts)
- Write Oasis House, PO Box 522, Grandview, MO 64030-0522

Go to www.oasishouse.com for special package discounts, book descriptions, ebooks, and free teachings.